DAYS IN DEVONPORT
Part I

Gerald W. Barker

Devonport Market and Garrison Town

These pictures help to show the blending of the military and civil life in the town. The eight faces of Devonport make up this composite postcard.

This version of the book is virtually as originally published, presenting the work of Gerald W Barker. There are now additional pages at the back providing information about the publisher, Arthur L Clamp.

The republishing project is being managed by Arthur's grandson, Steven Gibson. We aim to find all the research that he was involved in publishing, preserving it for the next generation as part of 'The Clamp Collection'.

INTRODUCTION

THE Carnival at Devonport Park, before the war, was one of the events well remembered by the people of Devonport. It started at Ker Street and made its way through Morice Square to the bandstand in Devonport Park. The carnival King would read a proclamation to the people, and the week's fun would begin. The proceeds would help such worthwhile causes as the Devonport Hospital which relied heavily on voluntary subscriptions. Entertainment was given to the crowds by the dedication of volunteers such as the Geraldine Lamb Dancers, who added to the gaiety in their white-pleated skirts and red coats.

The greatest danger to the boys and girls, playing in the streets around the park, came from the numerous handcarts in the vicinity. The fastest thing on two wheels was the Hovis-Bread cart, driven by Cyril. Games such as *Fly-boy, King* or *Weak-Horses* would come to an abrupt end when one of the trolleys (wooden boxes on four wheels) would be driven at breakneck speed past the Exmouth Hall, down Milne Villas, and into Ross Street, scattering boys and girls in all directions.

The Tivoli cinema, in Fore Street, was a favourite outing for many Devonport families. Mr. P. F. Ghillyer remembers the silent film era; he remembers, too, walking in "safari style" past the old Y.M.C.A., and the *Welcome*, with other cinema operators. The object of the exercise was to carry a full length feature film, plus the old Gaumont Graphic Newsreels, plus the two-reeler serial and a two-reeler comedy. After walking across Devonport Park with these films on their backs, they would take them to the Stoke Great Western Railway Station, and deposit them in the parcels office, which was open all night. The operators of the Tivoli, Electric, and Hippodrome Cinemas would then make their weary way past the Exmouth Hall to their homes.

Some of the grass of Devonport Park was later replaced by trenches in 1938 in preparation for the building of public air-raid shelters. A High-Explosive bomb that hit the corner of the shelter opposite Milne Place, but caused no casualties, provided the boys and girls of the neighbourhood with an unexpected bonus. The large crater that was formed made a first-class "wall-of-death" for the many cyclists that rode around its circumference with speed and enthusiasm.

Meeting and talking to Devonport people, has, in itself, made the gathering of material for this illustrated booklet worthwhile. Mr. Mandy Davis and Mrs. Phyllis Woods, better known in Stoke Village as Phyllis Davies, remembered, as I did, when a boy, the incident, during the war, when the huge lorry that operated the barrage balloon was lifted like a toy by the balloon, and having been carried across the Blockhouse, was dumped on the slope on the opposite side.

Having finished a swim at the old Swimming Baths at Mount Wise, Mr. R. Smith recalled, as I did, the delight of visiting the small shop at the top of *Blagdons Boats for Hire* to buy a delicious drink from a lady called Clare Fleming, whose maiden name was Bromley. The Vantis drink came from a futuristic looking glass bowl that fascinated numerous visitors to the shop with the swishing noises and cascades of bubbles that mysteriously followed the pulling of the handle.

Mr. E. Bradley, who was a captain in the army, and later Superintendent at the Devonport Methodist Central Hall when Reverend E. Lewis was the Minister, remembers the troops between the wars marching through the gates of Raglan Barracks on their way to Sunday morning church service outside the barracks.

Apart from those whom I have mentioned I would like to thank those who have recalled memories or loaned photographs. Among these are Mr. F. W. Rowe, Mr. and Mrs. D. Newton, Mr. E. Drake, Mr. C. F. J. Soulsby, Mr. Devereux, Mrs. L. Burt, Mrs. E. High, Mr. D. Chamberlain, Mr. T. Rundle, Mr. C. Hambly, Mr. J. Williams, Mrs. White, Mr. R. Tozer, Mrs. Williams, Mr. E. Sutton, Reverend Grigg, Minister of Devonport Central Hall, Mrs. C. Cox, Mrs. Puckey, and J. R. Elliott, Area Librarian.

In preparation for *Days in Devonport*, Part II, I would be grateful for the loan of any photographs of old Devonport, particularly of the Devonport Carnival. Anyone that has any material in their possession, and would be willing to loan such is invited to contact me.

Finally, I wish to thank Arthur L. Clamp for his skill and enthusiasm in the field of illustration and for his help in the compiling of *Days in Devonport*.

Gerald W. Barker,
44 Burnham Park Road,
Peverell, Plymouth
September, 1982.

Tivoli Cinema

Admission for the "Tivoli" Cinema was 3d., 6d. and 9d. plus a shilling for the best six rows of red plush seats at the back. The name *Tivoli* was derived from the fact that the beautifully designed post office, a few yards away had been copied from the Tivoli in Rome. Harry Harcourt allowed the unemployed to see the shows for 3d. on production of their yellow card.

York Street School

Len Harvey, the ex-Champion Heavyweight boxer, was a pupil at York Street School, formerly known as *Cherry Garden Street School*. He is in the second row from the back and six in from the right. A plaque in the assembly hall gave details of their famous pupil. The headmaster in 1918 was Mr. Elliott (left). The arches later became the entrances to the air raid shelters.

St. Stephen's Infant School

This is a group of pupils at the infants school of St. Stephens, near Pembroke Street. The Headmistress was Mrs Reed, who is on the right of the picture.

"Poor Man's Corner"

Richmond Walk or "poor man's corner", as it is known to older Devonport people, was the 'gateway' to the lower part of lovely Mount Wise. The house boats provided many an onlooker on Stonehouse Bridge or "half-penny gate", as it was called, with much pleasure.

Mount Wise Signal Station

The Signal Station at the top of Mount Wise was well known to the sailors at sea, and to those that worked inside it. Bullocks Dock once had a sausage factory in its vicinity and a coal store. It was situated in the area now occupied by the new swimming baths.

Commander in Chief's Boathouse

The building, surrounded by water was the Commander in Chief's boathouse. Rowing boats for staff would be "housed" there. Just out of range was moored the C. in C.'s yacht *Vivid*. Gordon Campbell, V.C., who was in charge of the "Q" ships during the Great War, lived in one of the houses.

Mount Wise Swimming Baths

The "Old" Swimming Baths at Mount Wise, which were reached by descending the steep set of steps, were free to men and boys. After boys had completed "land drill" by "swimming" on a chair they faced reality when they entered the water and encountered Captain Carter, whose instruction taught many boys to swim. Canadian army engineers, in later years, filled in the old swimming baths.

Admiral's Hard, Stonehouse

Looking across to Mount Wise from Admiral's Hard a train is seen standing at Ocean Quay. French strawberries would be landed from one of many ships and then transported to London by the South Western Railway Company.

Mount Wise from Cremyll Head

The large building on the left puzzled many of the older citizens of Devonport as to its usage. Mr Jack Williams, eighty years old of Pasley Street, remembers it as a hall that was once used as a games court. The word "Rackets" was written on a large board and this was visible to walkers. In its earlier days the building served as an army drill shed.

Fore Street, Devonport, 1938

This roughly drawn list of businesses flourishing in Fore Street will recall the busy days of 1938 when it was compiled. All the names were well known to local people and the street was seldom empty of busy shoppers, sailors off duty or people coming and going to work in the Yard. The blitz, of course, blotted out this prosperous street of shops but their way of life, ranges and prices still linger on in the minds of many local people. The following pages show various views of this part of Devonport.

Fore Street Blitz Survivor

The Western Railway Tavern is one of the few Fore Street buildings that remained standing after the air raids of 1939–44. A few yards away from the tavern during the period of the war the strains of Glen Miller's records could be clearly heard by passers-by in Fore Street. The "yankees" were at home in Raglan Barracks.

GRANBY BARRACKS

No.	Business
119	Norman Campbell Confectioner
117	E.C. Knit Wear Wool Shop
117	Albert Pengelly Ltd. Tobacconist's
117	Mrs K. Driscoll Confectioner
	The Electric Theatre

HIGH ST

116	Military Hotel P.H.
115	Hocking Pianos
114	Site for Forum Cinema
110	Singers
109	David Greig
108½	Leon Prior Fleur / John Song Dyers
108	
107	Hearne's Miller
106	Salmon & Gluckstein

ST. AUBYN ST.

105	Millbay Hotel Clnrs
104	Owen Baker
103	
102	Marks & Spencer
101	
100	
99	Midland Bank
98	J & M Stone
97	Montague Burton
96	

LAMBERT ST.

95	Patricks Vaults
94	Liptons
93	Tim White
92	H. Williams Penny Goods
91	Golden Lion P.H.
90	Western News
89	G. Bateman Opt
88	Two Trees
87	Coombes
86	
85	J.C. Tozer
84	

MARLBOROUGH ST.

83	Hepworths
82	British Home Stores
81	

MORICE STREET

78	Coombes Iron Mngr
77	Royal Hotel
76	Towlson Newsagt
75	Jean & Phinty Wine
74	Payne's Vaults

KING ST.

73	Barclays Bank
71	New London Inn
68	Sydney Lane Jn
67	
66	Dining Rooms
65	David Sale Ltd
63	Ironmongers
62	Mrs F. Waller Confectioner

FORE STREET (east side)

Business	No.
London & South Western Railway Tavern	1
Methodist Central Hall	
Welcome Buildings	2
Salmons (A & W Eustace) Newsagents	1
Madame Gertrude Ladies Hairdresser	2
Welcome Hall of Institute	2
Ainsworth Jn City Treasury	3
Devon Libraries Devonport	4
Railway Hotel	5
G. Widger Paint	6
Columbia Club	7
Tivoli Theatre	8
The Cottage V	9
Gas Showrooms	10

CHAPEL ST

Post Office	11
Reindeer Cycles	12
Co-op Society	13
Boots the Chemists	14

ST AUBYN ST.

Co-operative Society	16
London Silversmith	20
'H' versmith	21
Underwoods	22
Grocers	23

LAMBERT ST

Nat. Prov. Bank	24
Licensed House	25
True Form	26
Morris Radio	27
Richards Shoes	28
Currys Cycles	29
Lloyds Bank	30, 31
Snell & Co	32
Maypole Dairy	33
Geo Oliver	34, 35
J.C. Tozer	36, 37

TAVISTOCK ST.

Prince George P.H.	38
Wood & Tover	39
F.W. Woolworth	40, 41
Stead & Simpson	42
Stumbles Outf.	43
Pote & Sons Outfitter	44
Ley Tobcnst	45
E.E. Venn Butch	46
McSweeney (Fried Fish)	47
Wm Lamey (Fruit)	48
Speedy Shoe Service	49
Saccone & Speed Ltd	50
Spanish Vice-Consulate (E.G. Hathaway Vice Consul)	

CATHERINE ST.

| Royal Sailors Rest and Institute | 56, 59 |
| Dock Gates & Queen Street | |

RAGLAN BARRACKS

Early Fore Street

Much of Fore Street has changed. Horses and handcarts, however, remained part of the Devonport scene for many years later. In the 1930s milk was delivered by floats driven by horses. R. Cundy Dairies of Stoke had their stables where Penlee Secondary School is now situated. A giant milk churn on a float, owned by the Three Towns Dairy, would have its contents measured into jugs.

Commerce in Devonport

Devonport families found relaxation and much pleasure in looking at the Shops, beginning near the Dockyard Gate and finishing at the Shops adjacent to the Electric Cinema.

Royal Hotel, Fore Street

Fore Street would often be filled with sailors, who would be enjoying the public houses, shops, three cinemas, theatre or waiting for trams to take them to Plymouth. The *Royal Hotel* is on the left and was once noted for its splendid assembly rooms. The Queen of Roumania visited Devonport Alexandra Maternity Hospital in 1925. She stayed at this hotel.

The Market Close By
Many Plymothians came to do their shopping in Fore Street or in its vicinity. Devonport has a fine market, built in the Italian style, and a visit to the Alhambra theatre afterwards, towards the top of the hill in Tavistock Street, would have been an added pleasure to the day's events.

Devonport Cinemas
Apart from the Tivoli Cinema in Fore Street and the Electric Cinema, which was almost opposite, another fine cinema, the Hippodrome, was only a few yards away. It was originally built in 1902 as a variety theatre.

King George V Coronation
The flags are out in Fore Street for the Coronation of King George V. Boys and girls in schools at Devonport remember receiving souvenir mugs on such Royal occasions. J. C. Tozer had shops on both sides of Fore Street.

Dockyard Gates from Fore Street

Aggie Westons, the Royal Sailors Rest, is the large building on the far left. This was a second home to the many sailors who had spent, in some cases, two and a half years abroad on a Commission. The beds made a luxurious change to sleeping in hammocks in confined spaces on board ship.

Royal Sailors Rest overlooking Main Gates

How to get into the Dockyard after midnight when the forbidding gates were shut? A press on the bell would result in a small door being opened by a Dockyard policeman who would usually have a friendly word of greeting to the bell-ringer in uniform.

A close view of the Yard Gates

After leaving the pleasures of 'Civvy Street' behind him the sailor walking towards the Dockyard Gates would be soon entering a miniature town with its own 'business' life, including a railway engine and carriage to transport passengers from South Yard to North Yard.

Pembroke Street Carnival, 1928

It is carnival time in Pembroke Street in 1928. The carnivals began in the 1920s and were sponsored by the theatres and cinemas of Devonport to help the unemployed. The following week would have a pram derby as a final event.

Putty Philpotts, Carnival King

King of the Carnival was Putty Philpotts, who was ex-doorman of the Palace Theatre, and landlord of the *No Place Inn*. His Queen was Edith Mayne, landlady of *Granby Vaults*, Devonport. The man in the trilby hat is thought to be Mr. Cowan. He would aid the Carnival by playing a trumpet on the street corner.

The Carnival Cavalcade

As Putty Philpotts was twenty stone, he was usually driven by the largest cars, in style, by Harry Taylor. Various slogans would be seen in Pembroke Street. In 1928, the words *Devonport Arises* could be seen above the barber's shop, owned by Bert Pearson.

The Fruit Shop, Pembroke Street, 1928

The fruit shop in Pembroke Street belonged to the Drake family. In the picture, four generations are seen; Ernie Drake's father, sister, grandmother and nephew, Terry Matthews. The butcher's shop on the left belonged to George Pitcher. The car belonging to Ernie's father was a Morris Cowley, DR 2705.

Pembroke Rowing Club

Being so near to the water at Mutton Cove, rowing, for the local men, was a natural sport. Many cobblestones can still be seen in such places as the remains of Fort Street.

Pembroke A.F.C., 1912–13

Although many people in the area were unemployed and money was scarce, the inhabitants of Pembroke Street and district enjoyed the opportunities given them in the field of sport. Members of the Devon Junior League are seen here in 1912–13.

The Garrison Church

It was built in 1856 to serve the two regiments of the line consisting of 80 officers and 2,000 men. One of its earlier chaplains was the Rev. Dudley Somerville, M.A. The church stood on the opposite side of the Barracks. Mrs. Bradley, whose husband served in the Army, remembers worshipping in the building.

Sparrow Park, Devonport

Sparrow Park was a pleasant area at the bottom of Albert Road and to the left of the Dockyard Gates. The Salvation Army, having marched from their hall in Gloucester Street, would often play their instruments by the side of the park, outside the Dockyard Gates.

Some Devonport Men

Devonport men enjoying the outdoor life. It would be a brave man it seems who would dare to have been photographed without his cap on. Can readers identify any of them and the occasion?

Morice Town School in 1935

The author is seated on the extreme right with others remembered by him being Raymond Kellaway, Sylvia Ross, Sylvia Horne, Ken Oram (with the bandage), Dora Rothery, Fred Merrin, John Waterfield and Ralph Searle. Miss Beer was the headmistress and the headmaster of the juniors was Mr. Dunn. The school entrance was opposite Sambell's sweet shop in Charlotte Street which was also blitzed. Side entrances were in Albert Road a little way up the hill from the H.M. Naval Base entrance.

St. James the Great School Staff, c. 1910

The Staff of St. James the Great Junior School about 1910. Right of centre was Miss Jones. The Staff transport can be seen to the right of the group. In the 1930's the Headmaster was Mr. Nelson and some of the teachers were: Mr. Bailey, Mr. Southgate, Mr. Birch and Miss Beer.

Somerset Place School Class

Somerset Place School, as it was once known, had, as so many schools of the period did, some of the windows in the classroom high up from the floor. This ensured the pupils would not be distracted from outside. John Oliphant is in the second row, fourth from the right.

Devonport Guildhall and Column

Foulston, the architect, would not have approved if he had known his magnificent Devonport Guildhall would one day have been the centre for some of the people of Devonport to collect their gas masks in 1939. The story of the statue, that never was, on top of the column, to the left of the Egyptian House, is well known to the locals. This engraving dates from about 1830 and shows the area a few years after the column was erected in 1823 at a cost of £2,750.

This commemorative iron plate recalls the year when the town adopted its new name in 1824. It still stands close to the base of the column. The much later circular wall plaque gives further particulars of this part of the history of the town. The Guildhall was built during 1821–22 at a cost of £3,000.

Ker Street Infants' School, 1903

A short cut from the middle of Pembroke Street to Ker Street could be taken by walking in the direction of Ker Street Ope, and under the "tunnel" of houses. Mr. Ernie Drake, the grocer, had his stores at the bottom of Ker Street Ope, after being blitzed out of Devonport Market.

Commemorative Plaque

John Wesley would not have approved of the pioneers of the Salvation Army in Devonport being locked up in the police station at the rear of the Guildhall. This plate recalls another interesting part of the long story of the old borough.

Ker Street Chapel, 1785

This solitary engraved stone is the only remains of Devonport's large chapel which was visited by John Wesley in 1746. His reception in the area was often initially very tempestuous but through his work Methodism was born and developed a strong local following.

The Old Chapel Inn

Formerly a non-conformist place of worship it later became a wine store. It bears the date 1790 and was used by Dockyard workers who were Unitarians. Nearby Cumberland Gardens was the site of a theatre and on the opposite side of the gardens boys would run after the trams and jump on their "backs" as they made their way up into Chapel Street.

C. B. Courtenay Thomas.
Accountant and Auditor, Devonport.

Who well looked after the Ratepayers interest in showing up overcharges and illegal payments when auditing the Devonport Corporation accounts, and endured any amount of persecution for so doing.

C. B. C. Thomas, Devonport. No. 2.

A Devonport Character

One of the well-known characters of Devonport was C. B. Courtenay Thomas. He was an accountant and auditor, who well looked after the ratepayers' interest, in showing up overcharges and illegal payments when auditing the Devonport Corporation accounts, and endured any amount of persecution for so doing.

Pennycross Bill, about 1900

Pennycross Bill was a Three Towns character, and well known to the people of Devonport about 1900. Another character in the 1930's was "Colonel". He lived near Morice Town School and was well known to boys and girls and popular in Devonport Park during carnival week.

The Jolly Sparkers

The Jolly Sparkers were one of many groups that helped to enliven the Devonport scene. Individuals, too, such as Mr. Albert Haderly, would play on a banjo to the car queues at Torpoint Ferry, and also do some "busking" to the Devonport cinema queues. Can anyone recognize the players?

Devonport Park

The grassed area around the bandstand would be covered by people sitting down enjoying the fresh air. The circular path around the top of the park, called the *Oval*, would be full of people who were relaxing, by walking around it. The park was laid out in 1858 and then covered thirty seven acres of land.

Devonport Park

The part of the park near the Brickfields had tennis courts and another bandstand. Mr. Mandy Davis of Stoke village remembers listening to musicians performing in it. During the last war American troops "dug in" in the park and billets were erected for their accommodation for the greater part of the hostilities.

A Tram at Stoke Damerel

Although Stoke Damerel Church looks peaceful, apart from the transient noise of the tram, it was, at one time, situated in a sinister environment. Until 1827 a Gibbet stood on the opposite side of the road to the church. Richards and W. Smith were executed for the murder of Mr P. Smith, a clerk in the Dockyard in 1787.

Royal Naval Barracks, Devonport

Many of the sailors from the barracks gained increased respect from the people of Devonport by their fire-fighting and rescue actions during the heavy air raids. They suffered many casualties themselves when the R.N. Barracks was hit by bombs. This view of the barracks was taken from a set showing different barracks in the area and date around the turn of the century.

Inside the Barracks

"Remember to salute the quarterdeck, when you get inside those gates, and always salute the band when it's marching through the barracks, because there will be an officer with it." This was sound advice for any sailors "visiting" the barracks for the first time.

Raglan Barracks, Devonport, built 1853

"I'm going to the Lines", would mean simply going to the Raglan Barracks, to the locals. Company after company of soldiers would be seen by Devonport men and women, boys and girls on Sunday mornings, as the soldiers marched on the huge parade ground in preparation for the military bands to lead them to church.

The Parade Ground

On Sundays the soldiers would play their musical instruments to the delight of citizens of all ages. They would alternate each Sunday as to whether it was the north part of the parade ground or the south part. Not far away, on the Brickfields site, many local lads enjoyed seeing Sergeant Joe Louis, heavy weight champion of the world, spar with Sergeant Joe Nicholls of New York.

Admiralty House, Mount Wise

This stands near the site of Captain R. F. Scott, R.N., the Devonport born explorer's statue. At the beginning of the last war Mount Wise was the centre in the fight against the U-boats and has always been an important building to Devonport and to the nation. This early view of the building shows it in its original form many years ago. The locality is named after Sir Thomas Wise.

Local Defence Volunteers

A section of the local Devonport L.D.V. as it was then known before becoming the Home Guard. A call was made for volunteers with war experience. The three on the left are Dockyard workers; Mr. Tex Rundle of the Hon. Artillery Company is here, an ex-stoker R.N. and the C.O. was Captain Humphrey Woolcombe of Hemerdon House.

Post Office Guard Duty

The L.D.V. was responsible for night time guard duty at the G.P.O. in Fore Street. The entrance to the guard room was a few yards down Chapel Street. The six men on duty each had a rifle but they only had one clip of five rounds of .303 ammunition between them. This passed from hand to hand at hourly intervals!

Marlborough Street

Swiss, the toy shop, was the most popular shop in this once very busy area of Devonport. This view will undoubtedly bring back many memories including late night shopping on Saturday in order to get cheap joints of meat for the Sunday dinner. Note the *Revenue Inn* on the right.

A Day's Outing

The introduction of the old styled char-a-banc during the 1920's gave rise to all sorts of day excursions for local people. Here a group pose outside the Liberal Club, 9 St. Aubyn Street,

Marlborough Street

The lamp on the corner, as well as many others in Devonport, was lit by a man each evening going from one to another with a light at the top of a long pole. The lamplighter, as he was called, inserted the pole through a flap near the glass to ignite the small jet of gas. Note the absence of vehicles in this very early scene of the street.

Merrymaking at Camp

The musical instruments here certainly date this photograph but unfortunately no names have been forthcoming about the people. There were many occasions for self entertainment years ago and this is a very typical scene of those days.

Torpoint Ferry

The ferry "on chains" has transported thousands of people from Devonport to Torpoint or "Tar Point", as it was once called because of the sailing ships that went there from Devonport Dockyard to be tarred. Considering the volume of traffic in Civil and Naval ships passing to and fro, there have been few accidents involving the ferry.

Alighting from the Ferry

Mothers from Devonport, who were unable to afford trips to the moors or seaside, would push their prams on to the ferry and, having paid one penny at the turnstile on the Torpoint side, would spend a pleasant day on the "Lawn". In those days the oil tanks were well hidden.

Victoria Royal, 1847

This engraved stone is the keystone of a small arch below Mount Wise and commemorates the buildings at the waterfront put up here in that far off period. The limestone has weathered very well as it faces away from the sea. The entrance now leads to the open air swimming pools and to the boat yard to the east.

Mayor of Devonport, 1910

Alderman Littlejohn, J.P., proudly poses for the camera at the proclamation of the King George V on the 10th May, 1910. The old borough had its mayor and corporation for many years before amalgamating with Plymouth in 1914.

Coronation Medal

The wording on this Edward VII commemorative medal reads: The County Borough of Devonport June 26th 1902. The Mayor: Edgar M. Leest. The faces are those of Queen Alexandra and King Edward VII.

Richard's Shop

This shop has not been identified yet but it has a number of interesting items on display with prices. Shaving 3d., haircutting, shampooing and singeing were 6d. Those were the days! Presumably the proprietor and his wife are the two people in the entrance.

The Alhambra Theatre

The lady holding the handbag is Mrs. Edith Rice, the wife of the proprietor of the once popular Alhambra. Mr. Clarry Hambly, who was the stage manager of the theatre which opened in 1924, remembers the wagonettes from Mutton Cove advertising the programmes on the sides of the vehicles. The blitz closed a chapter on the old times of Devonport part of which was this well remembered theatre.

Outside the Alhambra

Mr. Bert West, the manager, is on the left of the picture. Edith Rice is behind the dog. Wallie Rice, the proprietor, standing centre is reputed to have nearly always been smoking cigarettes. Stall prices were 2/6d., pit 1/3d., circle 2/- and gallery 5d. The theatre was opened by Colonel Bastard at Easter, 1924, for revue and vaudeville productions. Mrs. Wagner's operatic company were among the first performers here.

A Family Group

The boy standing behind the dog is Dennis Newton. His aunt, Mrs. Edith Rice, is standing behind him. In the centre is Mrs. Flora Newton and Mr. Charles Frederick Newton who was the manager of the bars. Can anyone identify the word on the background starting with the letter P?

Arthur L. Clamp – the man behind the books

Arthur Leslie Clamp was a man of boundless energy with a passion for helping others, particularly through his love of history. A printer by trade, he started his career in a printing company before moving his family from Exeter to Plymouth to teach at the Plymouth College of Art and Design, where he eventually became the Head of the Printing Department.

A Devoted Family Man

Despite his love of teaching, Arthur prioritised his family, always making it home by 5:30pm for tea. He and his wife, Rosemary, raised five children: Susan, Angela, Elizabeth, David, and Steven. Arthur would often combine his love of family and history by taking his children on Sunday walks, encouraging them to appreciate historical monuments by taking photos or making crayon rubbings of gravestones for his books. The family home at 203 Elburton Road was a hub of activity, with a large garden, featuring a two-storey fort and a makeshift swimming pool.

Arthur with his five children.

A Lifelong Learner and Adventurer

Arthur's thirst for knowledge extended beyond history to a deep curiosity about the world. He was passionate about exploring different cultures, traditions, and cuisines, often taking advantage of his long summer holidays as a teacher to travel to places like India, Russia, South America, the middle east and the USA, sometimes bringing one of his children along. This adventurous spirit even influenced his home life, as seen by the short-lived family tradition of steam-cooking vegetables after a trip to Iceland.

History is a prominent feature of family days out

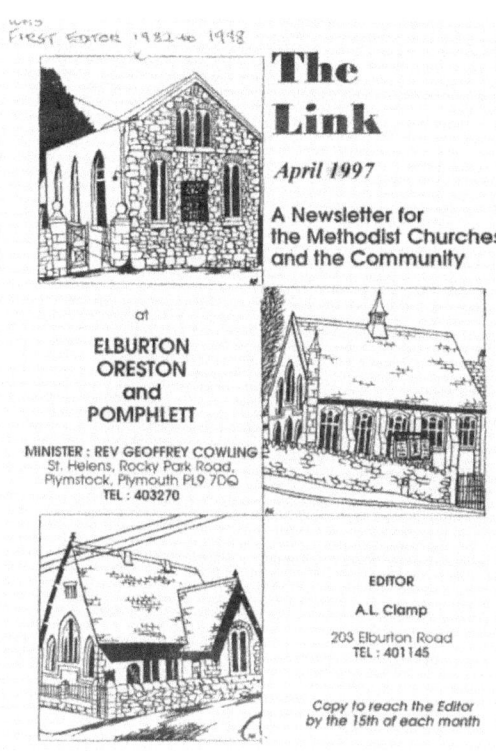

Community and Philanthropic Spirit

His commitment to serving others was evident in his long-standing involvement with the Elburton Methodist Church. He was the Sunday School Superintendent for over 15 years and served as the editor of the wider church's monthly newsletter, "The Link," for a similar duration. After Rosemary's very sad passing, Arthur later remarried and, following a chance encounter with a professor from India, established a connection with a missionary school in Chennai. Together with his new wife, Christine, he co-founded a "Sponsor a Child's Education" program that continues to this day.

Pictured left – The cover of 'The Link' complete with hand drawn sketches of each church by Angela
Below right – Arthur Clamp promoting his latest book
Below left – Arthur at home with his first wife, Rosemary
Below centre – Arthur on holiday with his second wife, Christine

A Legacy of Learning and Positivity

Arthur's greatest passion was history, which he brought to life through tireless research, documentation, and the many books he authored. He was driven by a need to "never be stuck in a rut," constantly seeking new experiences, meeting new people, and expanding his knowledge. With a positive attitude and a great sense of humour, he was always ready to help others, leaving a lasting impact on his family and community. His children, Susan, Angela, Elizabeth, David, and Steven, remember him with love and gratitude.

David Clamp, 2025

A Legacy of Local History

Below is the story of how Arthur L Clamp began writing books, in his own words, drafted shortly before he passed away in 2001. I have only made minor alterations to this text, correcting grammatical errors that he did not survive to correct himself. When I first discovered this text, I was shocked to see my name mentioned. It seems that, unbeknownst to me, I shared my first PC with him. I suspect he used it during the day when I was at school, although I do have one memory of sitting with him and showing him how it worked. It has been a pleasure to pick up where he left off and see his books republished and redistributed, and to know that I was part of the story, even back then. It was also fascinating to discover that his pricing structure matches the way I have tried to price the books, with a third going to local sellers and the rest covering printing costs with a little left over for my expenses.

I am his eldest grandson, and it is a privilege to curate his legacy, which we are calling 'The Clamp Collection'. The very last line of the text originally reads "The following pages list all the titles." Sadly, that page is missing and we have no record of all the books he published and knowing that some of those were researched by other authors makes the process of finding them even harder. I look forward to one day completing the collection and seeing them all available again. And maybe, one day, I'll even start writing my own to add to the series. For now, here is his story in his own words.

Steven Gibson, 2025

Writing and Publishing Booklets on Local Topics and Areas

I started this interest in either 1968 or 1969 when living in Woodford. I had by these dates established the Department of Printing and I think I must have been looking for something different to do. The first titles were of A5 size proofed from type set at Clarke, Doble and Brendon, Ltd., Plymouth printers, and then made up into pages and printed at Sawtell and Neilson, Ltd., Totnes.

Then began a slow process of getting them out to shops, etc. which proved to be more time consuming and difficult than actually researching, writing and getting the books into print. However, I persisted and opened a business account with Barclays Bank on the Broadway. I was advised to give it a title so I called it "Westway Publications". There came along another problem, one of storage of paper and finished books which was solved when the family moved to Elburton in 1970.

I changed the printer to Penwell, Ltd., Callington, Cornwall, as he was then just setting up himself and his prices seemed very reasonable. I did not get any of the printers to make up the complete books. I hand folded the flat printed sheets, stitched the books on a small manual table stitcher and trimmed them in a small hand turned guillotine which I bought from someone in Penzance for £40. It was brought up in a van.

The trouble and time going to and fro to Callington was too much so I transferred the printing to PDS Printers, Prince Rock, Plymouth, and I have been with them ever since. Now they are at Plympton which is easy to reach and they fold the flat sheets which was turning out to be a long chore which only saved a small part of the printing costs.

All my first titles were written by myself. I took the photographs and developed them in the loft of the house, the type was set by now on a computer situated in the house at Elburton from which I had collected photographic lengths of text to cut up and law down as pages.

At some point I decided that I would do my own film processing of lith film so I bought a large second hand process camera from Kingsbridge and learnt through trial and error to make line negatives of the text and halftone negatives of the illustrations which proved more difficult than I anticipated. The main problem was trying to keep the developer in the large dish at the correct temperature as any change would affect the developing time. I replaced this old camera with a brand new one bought from Croydon, Surrey, costing £900. This has turned out to be a great asset cutting out an expensive part of the printer's costs and one crucial aspect of the work which I could control.

By the middle 1970s there were many outlets I had contacted in Plymouth, up to Dartmoor, Exeter, around to Torbay, Totnes, Dartmouth and the South Hams. The market for local books was much greater than I had first thought and through getting to know many local people undertaking research themselves had the chance to help and make up books for other people who had in most instances, got together a collection of photographs with some text in a rather muddled way. Through my experience in print I was able to shape up their work and get it into print and in every case I had to pay the printer and let the person have the royalties. In the majority of titles produced in this manner this was another way of producing titles and it did give some profit to my work. However, I must say that in a few cases I lost out by either the other person getting the numbers wrong, not returning any monies from stock I delivered or they thought that more of their books should have been sold.

The print run was usually 1,000 copies and from time to time I have had reprints of 250 copies. It took about ten years to clear the first print run so I always had large stocks in the garage, workshop, etc. The numbers sold during the early years was about 7,000 copies a year increasing to around 9,000 copies and for the whole of the enterprise about 500,000 have been sold. The booklets have become part of the local scene and many people collect them, shops regularly order copies and I go around certain areas month by month restocking or replacing titles as necessary.

During the past year or so I have started setting the text on a Packard Bell PC, something which I should have done some years back. I share it with Steven Gibson, my grandson. There appears to be no end to the market for local books, but I could not earn a regular income because of the long time it takes to sell stock.

However, now exceeding 100 titles made up mainly of A4 twenty-four page booklets, some folded guides, with selling prices set with a third going to the shop which is the trade custom, the original idea has been quite successful and could go on for ever.

Apart from monetary benefits, however spasmodically these might be, I have learnt a lot myself, met many interesting people and have become part of the local scene with requests to give talks and to advise people about getting into print.

Arthur L Clamp, 2001

Death of local historical author

'He was an incredible character who was just loved by everybody who knew him'

A WELL-loved Elburton author has died at the age of 68.

Arthur Clamp (pictured right), who was one of the West Country's most successful writers, died at St Luke's Hospice, Turnchapel, after losing his battle against cancer.

Tributes have been flooding in for a man who was known in the community as a prominent writer and outgoing person.

He produced more than 140 titles during his life, dealing with both fiction, fact and history, often discussing West Country topics that were close to his heart.

One of his most acclaimed books was *The Plymouth Blitz*, and he also won credit for *The Rise and Fall of the Bearings of Membland Hall*, set in Noss Mayo.

He achieved sales of between 7,000 and 9,000 books every year and it is estimated that he has sold over half a million books, covering the areas of Plymouth, Dartmoor, Exeter, Torbay and the South Hams.

Mr Clamp was born in Mitcham, Surrey, in 1932, and was the eldest of four children.

He moved to Devon in 1941 to avoid the London air-raids.

Mr Clamp trained as a printer in Exeter and also gained a teachers' certificate in 1959 from Garnet College in London.

Plymouth College of Art, however, was to prove to be Mr Clamp's working home for the following 32 years until 1991, when he retired as head of the printing department.

He had a great interest in travel and had visited the USA, Tanzania, China, Russia, Peru, as well as travelling across Europe, where he presented talks and slide-shows on his experiences as a writer.

Mr Clamp was a member of Elburton Methodist Church for many years, superintendent of the Sunday school and editor of the church newsletter, as well as being involved in much charity work.

He was president of the Plymouth and District Field Club and an active member of the Elburton Residents' Association.

He enjoyed leading walks on Dartmoor and historical tours throughout the West Country.

Mr Clamp married his first wife, Rosemary, in 1956 and they had five children - Susan, Angela, Elizabeth, David and Steven - and she died in 1987. He also had 11 grandchildren.

He leaves a wife Christine, after remarrying in 1991, and her two children and three grandchildren.

'He was an incredible character who was just loved by everybody who knew him,' said his wife.

'He will be missed by his family, his friends, the people he worked with and just everybody who knew him through his books.'

More than 300 mourners attended his funeral at Elburton Methodist Church on Monday.

The attendance was a celebration of his life – he would have found that really special. It shows his vibrancy and love of people,' said Mrs Clamp.

Steven Clamp added that his father was 'a well respected and loved man, missed by a great many people throughout the South West and far beyond'.

This newspaper article, published by the Evening Herald on 17th August 2001, forms a good record of his life. Just as he encourages us to learn more about local history, we encourage you to learn a little about him. For that reason, we have included these pages at the back of all the most recently republished books, in honour of his memory and recognition of his contribution to the community.

www.ingramcontent.com/pod-product-compliance
Lightning Source LLC
Chambersburg PA
CBHW061406070526
44584CB00031B/4176